SEVEN WORDS
LEADER GUIDE

SEVEN WORDS
LISTENING TO CHRIST
FROM THE CROSS

Seven Words

978-1-7910-0781-2

978-1-7910-0782-9 ebook

Seven Words: DVD

978-1-7910-0785-0

Seven Words: Leader Guide

978-1-7910-0783-6

978-1-7910-0784-3 ebook

SEVEN WORDS

LISTENING TO CHRIST FROM THE CROSS

Susan Robb

Leader Guide
by Randy Horick

Abingdon Press | Nashville

SEVEN WORDS
LISTENING TO CHRIST FROM THE CROSS
LEADER GUIDE

ISBN-13: 978-1-7910-0783-6

20 21 22 23 24 25 26 27 28 29 — 10 9 8 7 6 5 4 3 2 1
MANUFACTURED IN THE UNITED STATES OF AMERICA

CONTENTS

INTRODUCTION

In *Seven Words: Listening to Christ from the Cross,* Susan Robb invites readers to listen to the final words of Jesus's life in a new way—a way that can be both challenging and empowering.

As the book's title suggests, the Gospels record only seven utterances from Jesus during the six hours he spent on the cross. No individual Gospel, however, includes more than three of these utterances, and Matthew and Mark each mention only one. Thus, in reading the passion narrative of Jesus's arrest, suffering, and death from only one Gospel, readers are unable to consider the totality of Jesus's last words, and they may see them more as details in the story than as statements with richer meaning for our lives.

In the book, Robb shows that Jesus's words from the cross, taken together, allow us to see the broad arc of Jesus's ministry and teaching. They offer us an intimate portrait of Jesus's humanity and of his relationship to the Father. They contain a powerful display of forgiveness and offer a glimpse of the inclusiveness of God's kingdom. They reveal that, even on the cross, Jesus teaches about the new kind of relationships—families defined by belief rather than blood—that he has called into being. And they show us Jesus's understanding of, and faithfulness to, the mission that God gave him. Robb shows us how each of these last words connects to themes established earlier in Jesus's ministry, and she provides the scriptural context that gives readers a much deeper appreciation of what Jesus was really saying.

Most of all, she invites readers to lean in and listen not just to what Jesus is saying in response to those around him on that fateful day, but to each of us, here and now—and to hear how those words can bring us into more faithful, committed discipleship in our journey through Lent and beyond.

This Leader Guide is designed to help Christian adult education leaders guide a group through a six-session Lenten study of Jesus's final words, a study informed by Robb's book. The guide contains quotations from her book that can serve as prompts for discussion, but groups will gain the most when the guide is accompanied by reading both *Seven Words* and the Gospel narratives of Jesus's arrest, trial, and crucifixion.

ABOUT THE SESSIONS

Here is an overview of the six sessions in this Leader Guide:

- "Session 1: Father, Forgive Them" introduces participants to Jesus's final words, how they are presented in the four Gospels, and what they reveal about Jesus when we examine them together rather than individually. The session also leads participants to avoid the temptation of skipping the pain of the cross to reach the joy and triumph of Easter, keeping us focused on the meaning of what Jesus said. In exploring Jesus's words, "Father, Forgive Them," this session also will help participants place themselves at the scene, as co-conspirators in Jesus's crucifixion, making his appeal to God for radical forgiveness not just a one-time event but one offered on our behalf as well. The session will help participants understand that, as forgiven people, they are called to radical forgiveness.

- In "Session 2: Today You Will Be with Me in Paradise," participants will connect Jesus's experience on the cross to his temptation in the wilderness, pitting his human desire to be spared the cup of suffering against his faithfulness to the mission. The session also takes us behind the simple words of a criminal hanging next to Jesus to understand what he was really saying— and what Jesus said to him in turn.

- "Session 3: My God, My God" takes participants into the depth of Jesus's suffering—and into the time when they, too, may have felt abandoned by God. It also takes participants beyond the words

8

that form the title of the chapter to explore the fuller meaning of the scripture that Jesus quoted and its implications for our lives.

- In "Session 4: Woman, Here Is Your Son," participants will explore what Jesus was really saying, not just to his mother and one of his disciples but to all of his followers, then and today. Then participants will consider how Jesus calls his disciples into a different kind of family—and how they should use that call to see relationships with others in a new way.
- In "Session 5: I Am Thirsty," participants will go beyond Jesus's words to explore how he represented "living water" for those who are spiritually thirsty. They will also consider his words in the context of the message of the cross, when this source of living water was "poured out" for humankind—and what it means for disciples to live into this example.
- In "Session 6: Into Your Hands," participants will consider Jesus's words not as a statement of surrender and defeat but one of faithfulness and triumph. In so doing, they will explore their own sense of mission as disciples and what it means to entrust their lives and spirit into God's hands.

Each of the six session plans includes:

- Stated goals to keep in mind as you lead discussions.
- The printed text, from the New Revised Standard Version (NRSV), of the portion of Jesus's words from the cross discussed in that session. (Sessions contain additional scripture texts, as well, and all sessions refer participants to other passages in several discussion questions.)
- Extensive discussion questions to facilitate participants' engagement with both the biblical text and *Seven Words*. You likely won't have time or desire to use all of the questions; choose the ones most interesting and/or relevant to your group.
- Opening and closing prayers to ground your sessions in an atmosphere of worship.

Some sessions contain optional, easy-to-prepare, and easy-to-do activities to serve as "icebreakers" or interactive introductions to the session's topic. The use of a markerboard or flip chart is suggested for some of the discussions. Each session's "Suggested Leader Preparation" section will alert you to any extra materials you need to gather or preparation you need to do.

May God, in great grace, use this guide and your group's study to draw you closer to the cross—and closer to Jesus's words to you.

Session 1
FATHER, FORGIVE THEM

SESSION GOALS

This session's reading, discussion, reflection, and prayer will equip participants to:

- Consider what Jesus's words from the cross mean when taken together rather than individually.
- Resist the temptation to skip over the pain and shame of the Crucifixion story to focus on the joy of Easter.
- Recognize themselves as participants in Jesus's betrayal and Crucifixion.
- Understand and apply Jesus's example of radical forgiveness.
- Appreciate the radical nature of Jesus's call for God to forgive his killers even as they were in the act of killing him.
- Understand how "Father, forgive them" applies to all of those who helped bring about Jesus's crucifixion—and to us.
- Appreciate the power of forgiveness to transform lives—including the lives of those who forgive.

BIBLICAL FOUNDATIONS

Two others also, who were criminals, were led away to be put to death with him. When they came to the place that is called The Skull, they crucified Jesus there with the criminals, one on his right and one on his left. Then Jesus said, "Father, forgive them; for they do not know what they are doing." And they cast lots to divide his clothing.
Luke 23:32-34

11

"Love your enemies, do good to those who hate you, . . . pray for those who abuse you. . . .

"If you love those who love you, what credit is that to you? For even sinners love those who love them. . . . But love your enemies, do good. . . . Your reward will be great, and you will be children of the Most High; for he is kind to the ungrateful and the wicked. Be merciful, just as your Father is merciful."

Luke 6:27-28, 32, 35-36

Then Peter came and said to him, "Lord, if another member of the church sins against me, how often should I forgive? As many as seven times?" Jesus said to him, "Not seven times, but, I tell you, seventy-seven times.

"For this reason, the kingdom of heaven may be compared to a king who wished to settle accounts with his slaves. When he began the reckoning, one who owed him ten thousand talents was brought to him; and, as he could not pay, his lord ordered him to be sold, together with his wife and children and all his possessions, and payment to be made. So the slave fell on his knees before him, saying, 'Have patience with me, and I will pay you everything.' And out of pity for him, the lord of that slave released him and forgave him the debt. But that same slave, as he went out, came upon one of his fellow slaves who owed him a hundred denarii; and seizing him by the throat, he said, 'Pay what you owe.' Then his fellow slave fell down and pleaded with him, 'Have patience with me, and I will pay you.' But he refused; then he went and threw him into prison until he would pay the debt. When his fellow slaves saw what had happened, they were greatly distressed, and they went and reported to their lord all that had taken place. Then his lord summoned him and said to him, 'You wicked slave! I forgave you all that debt because you pleaded with me. Should you not have had mercy on your fellow slave, as I had mercy on you?'"

Matthew 18:21-33

SUGGESTED LEADER PREPARATION

- Before your first session, set aside enough time to read the narratives of Jesus's crucifixion from all four of the Gospels:

◊ Matthew 27:32-61
◊ Mark 15:16-41
◊ Luke 23:26-49
◊ John 19:16-30

Read the chapters in more than one translation (for example, New Revised Standard Version, New International Version, New American Bible Revised Edition, *The Message*), including one you've never read before. Read these chapters aloud. Make notes on how these Gospel accounts differ and how they are the same. Try outlining the chapters and summarizing them in your own words. The more you immerse yourself in the scripture, the better prepared you will be to help participants study each of its parts in the context of the whole.

- Carefully and prayerfully read Luke 23:32-34, making notes of whatever grabs your attention, sparks new questions, or provides new insights. If desired, consult a trusted Bible commentary after you have read and reflected on the text yourself.
- Carefully read the "Introduction" and "Chapter 1: Father, Forgive Them" in *Seven Words: Listening to Christ from the Cross*, by Susan Robb. Note any material you need or want to research further before the session.
- Have on hand Bible dictionaries and concordances (and/or identify trusted online equivalents), a variety of Bible translations for participants to use (recommended), index cards, and pencils/pens. If you are in touch with the people likely to join you for these sessions, invite them to bring their own Bibles.
- If using the DVD (also available as streaming video) in your study, preview the session 1 segment and choose the best time in your session to view it.

AS YOUR GROUP GATHERS: ORIENT THE STUDY TOWARD LENT

Welcome participants. Ask them to introduce themselves and to talk briefly about what they hope to gain from this study of Susan Robb's

Seven Words. Be ready to talk about your personal interest in and hopes for the study. If no one mentions Lent specifically, ask participants why they chose to be part of a Lenten study. Invite them to discuss various ways they have observed Lent, both personally and as part of a faith community. Note how often Lenten observance is associated with giving up something (and how frequently this act is associated with self-improvement, such as giving up sweets).

Ask:

- Why do you think Lent, for so many Christians, has come to be associated with giving something up rather than with taking up something new?
- What practices might followers of Jesus consider adding to their lives (or increasing in their lives) during Lent?

Remind participants that during Lent, we remember the journey that took Jesus to the cross. But Jesus called us to make that journey, too, teaching that anyone who wished to be his disciple must take up their own cross and follow him.

Ask participants to devote time in thought and prayer during the coming week to what they would be willing to "take up" for Lent. Ask them to be prepared to write down their commitment on a card (which does not have be shared with others) when the group meets next.

Pray this prayer, or one in your own words:

O God, give us the courage to take up our own crosses and follow the way you have shown us. Give us the faith to keep going with you until the end. Give us the ears to lean in and truly listen so we may understand what you were telling us in those final hours on the cross. And give us the hearts to make those words part of our own faith experience and to live into the gospel so that our lives may be "good news" for others, especially those who have not felt included in the beloved community of your children. Amen.

FRAME THE STUDY AROUND THE CROSS

In the introduction to her book, Susan Robb writes that for much of her life she wanted to gloss over the painful story of Jesus's death on the cross and skip to the joyful story of Jesus's resurrection. Yet Jesus understood, as the Gospel narratives make clear, that his ministry inevitably would put him on a path that could only end at the cross (and that when Peter voiced opposition to such a result, Jesus called him "Satan" and a "stumbling block").

Ask:

- What do you think of when you think of the cross? What words and feelings come to mind?

Ask participants to recall hymns about the cross they know or have sung. Look up and read some of the words to several of the hymns that people mention, using either a hymnal that you have brought to the session or performing an internet search. Ask what message about the cross each of these hymns conveys.

Invite participants to share responses to this question:

- What stumbling blocks hinder you from taking up your own cross and following Jesus?

The Seven Words, Separately and Together

Provide participants with index cards and pencils or pens.

Ask:

- If you wanted to explain Jesus's life and ministry to someone who knew nothing of him and your explanation could include only three things that Jesus said, which statements would you choose?

Ask the group to write their three responses on the index card and then share them with everyone. Note both the differences and similarities in participants' responses. Then explain that you are using this exercise to lead into a conversation about why, as Susan Robb explains in her book, six of Jesus's seven utterances from the cross are unique to either the Gospels of Luke or John. Review these utterances and their Gospel source from the introduction to *Seven Words*.

Discuss:

- What do each of these individual utterances contribute to the picture we have of Jesus? What dimensions of him do they reveal?
- In including these words, what message do you think each Gospel writer was trying to convey to his particular community?
- Which of these utterances seem most characteristic of the image of Jesus you have traditionally had? Why?
- Which utterances seem least characteristic of your image of Jesus? Why?

SEEING OURSELVES AT THE CROSS

Remind participants that Susan Robb includes us among the "them" that Jesus calls on God from the cross to forgive. She writes:

> We help crucify Jesus when we get caught up in crowd mentality and say or condone things that go against what we profess to believe and are called to practice as Jesus's followers—things we would never say or condone if we were standing alone. We assist in crucifying Jesus when, like Pilate, we fail to stand up for what we know is right and rationalize to ourselves the doing of wrong. We crucify Jesus little by little when we fail to have regard for how our words and deeds harm others, putting our own interests above theirs....

Invite the participants to discuss these questions:

- Have you ever thought of yourself as being among those who crucified Jesus? Why or why not?
- How and where do you see Jesus being crucified today?
- One of Jesus's own disciples betrayed him into the hands of those who meant to kill him. Ten others deserted him after his arrest. The only disciple who followed him to his trial, Peter, three times denied knowing him. Only one disciple came to witness Jesus's crucifixion. As fellow betrayers of Jesus, we at least are in good company. When you examine yourself closely, where have you betrayed or denied knowing Jesus?

- What is Jesus saying from the cross to us, his crucifiers? What do you think he most wants us to hear?

AMAZING GRACE AND RADICAL FORGIVENESS

Use the following questions to lead participants in a discussion of the attitude of radical forgiveness displayed by Jesus from the cross.

- Read Matthew 18:21-33—a parable of two debtors. What makes the king's response to the first debtor's request for forgiveness shocking and radical? How does this make the first debtor's subsequent actions even more shocking?
- What does Jesus's statement to Peter that he must forgive not seven times but seventy-seven times suggest about the nature of forgiveness? Why should we keep forgiving someone who keeps wronging us over and over?
- How do Jesus's teachings about forgiveness inform his request, "Father, forgive them" from the cross?
- Which do you believe should come first—repentance or forgiveness? How does repentance open the door to forgiveness? How does forgiveness open the door for someone to repent?
- Why does Jesus ask God to forgive those responsible for crucifying him before they have had an opportunity to repent— in fact, while they were still in the act of killing him?
- Can you imagine a sin that would be impossible to forgive? If so, describe it.
- As Susan Robb tells the story, Corrie ten Boom, a survivor of Nazi concentration camps, said she had never experienced God's love as intensely as in the moment she forgave one of her Nazi guards. How is forgiveness liberating?

THE CROSS AND THE LYNCHING TREE

Explain:

Throughout *Seven Words*, written in 2020 amid protests across the United States over the killings of Ahmaud Arbery, Breonna Taylor,

George Floyd, and others, Susan Robb connects our calling as disciples with the work of racial justice and reconciliation. The cross is a powerful symbol of America's tortured racial history. The apostle Paul connected Jesus's crucifixion to being hung from a tree (Galatians 3:13). Black Christians in the US have long made the connection between the cross and trees from which the bodies of lynching victims were hung.

Ask:

- How do Jesus's words from the cross upon which we focus in chapter 1 of *Seven Words* speak to America's racial history? How do they speak to the present moment of racial reckoning?
- How do Jesus's words suggest a way forward beyond the present moment?
- What would churches need to do to pursue that way forward? What would your congregation need to do? What would you personally need to do?

CLOSING ACTIVITY

Remind participants that this is a Lenten study—a time to remember that Jesus calls us, as his disciples, to take up our own cross and follow him. Tell them that, each week, we will return to the question:

- In the coming week, where and how will you take up your cross?

Invite the group to discuss this question, then close with this prayer or one in your own words:

Lord, forgive us, for when we have sinned we have not fully understood the hurt we were causing and the damage we were doing, both to others and to ourselves. May your words from the cross lead us to recognize the magnitude of what we have done, and may the amazing grace you offered us while we were still in the act of injuring you liberate us to be debt-cancellers, to respond to your mercy by practicing mercy, to be instruments of your forgiveness in a world that so often seems unforgiving. Amen.

Session 2
TODAY YOU WILL BE WITH ME IN PARADISE

SESSION GOALS

This session's reading, discussion, reflection, and prayer will equip participants to:

- Appreciate how the taunting from his "adversaries" while he was on the cross brought Jesus into temptation like he faced in the wilderness.
- Understand what the criminal was invoking in calling Jesus by his name.
- Better understand the nature of God's kingdom.
- Reflect on how we are called to "remember" others as God's children and point the way to God's kingdom through our actions toward them.

BIBLICAL FOUNDATIONS

Two others also, who were criminals, were led away to be put to death with him. When they came to the place that is called The Skull, they crucified Jesus there with the criminals, one on his right and one on his left. Then Jesus said, "Father, forgive them; for they do not know what they are doing." And they cast lots to divide his clothing. And the people stood by, watching; but the leaders scoffed at him, saying, "He saved others; let him save himself if he is the Messiah of God, his chosen one!" The soldiers also mocked him, coming up and offering him sour wine, and saying, "If you are the King of the Jews, save yourself!" There was also an inscription over him, "This is the King of the Jews."

One of the criminals who were hanged there kept deriding him and saying, "Are you not the Messiah? Save yourself and us!" But the other rebuked him, saying, "Do you not fear God, since you are under the same sentence of condemnation? And we indeed have been condemned justly, for we are getting what we deserve for our deeds, but this man has done nothing wrong." Then [the criminal] said, "Jesus, remember me when you come into your kingdom." He replied, "Truly I tell you, today you will be with me in Paradise."

Luke 23:32-43

SUGGESTED LEADER PREPARATION

- Carefully and prayerfully read this passage and make notes of whatever grabs your attention most and sparks questions or new insights. If desired, consult a trusted Bible commentary.
- Carefully read "Chapter 2: Today You Will Be with Me in Paradise" in *Seven Words*. Note any material you need or want to research further before the session.
- Have on hand a variety of Bible translations and trusted study Bibles and commentaries for participants to use (recommended) and a markerboard or flip chart.
- If using the DVD, preview the session 2 segment and choose the best time in your session to view it.
- Prepare the candles that you will light during the activity in the "As Your Group Gathers" section.

AS YOUR GROUP GATHERS

Welcome participants. Ask those who attended the previous session to talk briefly about what in it most interested, challenged, or helped them.

Note that a key portion of this week's scripture passage begins with three words that sound like a prayer: "Jesus, remember me." Explain that many people today feel isolated, forgotten by neighbors, by society, by our leaders, even by God.

Invite participants to describe someone, either an individual or groups (such as those experiencing homelessness) who may have been treated as "forgotten." (Caution the group against using an individual's name and ask them, instead, to describe that person's situation.) As each individual or group of persons is mentioned, light a candle.

Give all an opportunity to lift up "forgotten people."

Then say:

- The criminal who hung beside Jesus on the cross spoke for many others in asking to be remembered in God's kingdom. As we work through this session, discussing this request and Jesus's response, let us think not only of the criminal but of all those our group has just lifted up.

Pray this prayer or one in your own words:

Lord, we long for your kingdom. Even though we know that you always remember us, we still yearn for that peace that comes through the assurance that you are right beside us. And just as we forgive others because you have forgiven us, teach us to remember others as you remember us. Amen.

TEMPTATION ON THE CROSS

Ask:

- Imagine that you had unlimited power and that you wanted to bring about a more just and peaceful world. If you could do only one thing to help bring about that result, what would you do? Why would you choose that particular action? What might happen as a result of your action that could work against your desired outcome?

Allow time for the group to discuss these questions.

Then ask:

- If you had to do something you knew was wrong in order to achieve a greater good, would it be worth it? Why or why not?

After participants have discussed this question, read aloud the story of Jesus's temptation in the wilderness from Luke 4:1-13.

Discuss:

- In each of the three temptations, what exactly was Satan (the adversary) asking Jesus to do?
- Why would they have been tempting for someone whose mission was to show others what it meant to live under God's rule?
- Why do you believe that Jesus resisted these temptations?
- How would yielding to these temptations have helped define the kind of Messiah Jesus was going to be?

Now, read aloud Luke 23:32-43.

Ask:

- As Susan Robb notes in *Seven Words*, Luke's account of Jesus's temptation ends with the ominous-sounding words that the devil "departed from him until an opportune time." How might Jesus's hanging on the cross represent that time of opportunity for the devil?
- How, from a certain point of view, might it have served to bring more people to worship Jesus as the Messiah had he yielded to this temptation?
- How would that have changed his mission?
- Have you even been publicly dared (or double-dared!) to do something that you already were tempted to do? Did being dared in front of others make it harder to resist the temptation? How might Jesus's own temptation have been increased by the taunts from religious leaders, soldiers, and one of the criminals to save himself and come down from the cross? How might these dares have increased Jesus's suffering?

THE FAITH OF THE SECOND CRIMINAL

Susan Robb suggests that the second criminal knew something about Jesus's ministry before they wound up next to each other on crosses. She speculates that he might even have been among the crowd who shouted "Hosanna" and welcomed Jesus into Jerusalem just five days earlier. Invite the group to imagine for a moment, as Rev. Robb does. Ask them to suggest ways that the criminal might have been exposed to Jesus's teaching and ministry during that final week in Jerusalem. (You may wish to consult the Gospel accounts of that week from Luke 19–22 and Matthew 21–26). What might the criminal have seen and learned about Jesus from these events that took place in and around Jerusalem? How might they have affected what he said to Jesus on the cross?

After the group has had an opportunity to discuss these questions, note that the Gospels describe four great professions of faith in Jesus as the Messiah. Ask participants if they can name them:

- Peter's declaration that Jesus is "the Messiah, the Son of the living God" (Matthew 16:16).
- Thomas's declaration, upon seeing the risen Jesus and touching the nail marks in his palms, "My Lord and my God!" (John 20:28).
- Martha's declaration at Bethany, where Jesus has come following the death of her brother Lazarus: "I believe that you are the Messiah, the Son of God, the one coming into the world" (John 11:27).
- The words of the second criminal: "Jesus, remember me when you come into your kingdom" (Luke 23:42).

If the group is unable to list all of these declarations, note the ones they did not name, and read each of the passages cited. Then focus participants' attention on the second criminal.

Ask:

- Were you surprised to hear of the criminal's words as a profession of faith? If so, why?
- What makes his words a statement of faith in Jesus? Be as specific as you can.

- The man admonishes his fellow criminal by asking, "Do you not fear God?" What does it mean to "fear" God? Fear of punishment? awe? reverence?
- How does Susan Robb suggest that the criminal's words make him a follower of Jesus the Messiah? What does this suggest about what it means to be a follower of Jesus?
- In Luke's Gospel, people often refer to Jesus as rabbi (or teacher) and Lord. But the thief is the only person to address Jesus by his name. As Rev. Robb points out, Luke surely wants us to notice this. But what, exactly, do you think Luke wants us to understand? What does this suggest about who Jesus is? about who the criminal is and what he is thinking? about our own relationship with Jesus?
- Read aloud Psalm 25:16-18, which includes a prayer to God by the psalmist to "remember me," along with these verses:

    Turn to me and be gracious to me,
    *   for I am lonely and afflicted.*
    Relieve the troubles of my heart,
    *   and bring me out of my distress.*
    Consider my affliction and my trouble,
    *   and forgive all my sins.*

    How does this psalm of David add to your understanding of the criminal's request to Jesus from the cross?

KINGDOM? PARADISE? TODAY?

Ask:

- When you hear the term "heaven" or "paradise," what words and images come to mind? How have we been acculturated to think of heaven? What makes it a paradise?
- As Susan Robb points out, our word for *paradise* comes from an ancient Persian word referring to the king's garden, like the Garden of Eden described in Genesis. What made that garden a paradise? List as many attributes as you can think of.

- When you hear the term "kingdom of God," what words and images come to mind? How are these similar to or different from the words and images you associate with paradise?
- How would you define the kingdom of God? (Use a markerboard or flip chart to list participants' responses for the whole group to see.)
- When the Pharisees question Jesus about when the kingdom of God is coming, he answers that it is already among them (Luke 17:20-21). Where do you see signs of the presence of God's kingdom? After the group has discussed this question, read aloud Luke 7:18-23, when John the Baptist's disciples ask Jesus whether he is the one they were expecting or whether they should wait for someone else. Jesus turns the question back on them and asks them to look around and describe what they have seen: "The blind receive their sight, the lame walk, the lepers are cleansed, the deaf hear, the dead are raised, the poor have good news brought to them" (v. 22). How do these signs define the nature of Jesus's messiahship and God's kingdom? Why do you think Jesus particularly emphasizes the poor as recipients of the good news of this kingdom? How does this passage affect your understanding of what the criminal is declaring when he affirms that Jesus is a king with a kingdom?
- What does it mean to live under God's kingship?

OPTIONAL ACTIVITIES

- Invite participants to use their cell phones to look up the meanings of their given names. Have them share their findings with the group. Then refer to the discussion in *Seven Words* about the meaning of Jesus's name ("he saves"). Use this as a springboard to examine the layers of meaning in the second criminal's choice to address Jesus by his name. Read aloud Luke 4:14-21.

Discuss:

> How did the well-known meaning of Jesus's name add greater meaning to his words at the end of this passage?

- Using your cell phones, invite the group to conduct a quick internet search using the words "cross display on a hill." Ask participants to share the images they find. If no one makes this observation, point out that the displays of crosses on a landscape invariably depict either a single cross or three crosses. Never are there only two crosses, even though only one of the criminals crucified alongside him became a follower of Jesus.

Discuss:

> What does this imagery suggest about the words "Remember me"? What does it suggest about whom we, as Jesus's followers, should remember? Why?

CLOSING ACTIVITY

Remind participants that this is a Lenten study—a time to remember that Jesus calls us, as his disciples, to take up our own cross and follow him. Invite them to respond to these questions:

- In the coming week, where will you take up your cross?
- Where will you show others a glimpse of God's kingdom?
- Where will you "remember" someone who may feel isolated, afraid, or emotionally wounded?

Say:

- God always remembers us, and God is always with us. But sometimes we need to be reminded, as the prophet Isaiah reminded the people during their time of exile in Babylon.

Read aloud to the group:

> *But now thus says the LORD,*
> *he who created you, O Jacob,*
> *he who formed you, O Israel:*
> *Do not fear, for I have redeemed you;*
> *I have called you by name, you are mine.*
> *When you pass through the waters, I will be with you;*
> *and through the rivers, they shall not overwhelm you;*
> *when you walk through fire you shall not be burned,*
> *and the flame shall not consume you.*
> *For I am the LORD your God,*
> *the Holy One of Israel, your Savior.*
> *I give Egypt as your ransom,*
> *Ethiopia and Seba in exchange for you.*
> *Because you are precious in my sight,*
> *and honored, and I love you.*

Isaiah 43:1-4a

Say:

- Just as we are Jesus's hands and Jesus's feet on earth, we also are called to be of the same mind as Jesus. We are called to reach out to show others that God remembers them, loves them, and acts through us to advance God's kingdom.

Pray this prayer or one in your own words:

Lord, we are your witnesses. We have witnessed how you remembered those who felt lost, those who were isolated, those who were suffering. Give us the strength and the resolve to take up our cross in remembering those around us who have not been treated fully as fellow children of God, so they may experience the peace of your kingdom that one day will come to all the world. Amen.

Session 3
MY GOD, MY GOD

SESSION GOALS

This session's reading, discussion, reflection, and prayer will equip participants to:

- Confront times in their own lives when they may have felt forsaken by God.
- Gain deeper insight into Jesus's humanity.
- Understand how a feeling of being forsaken by God affects the life of worshipping communities.
- Explore the fuller meaning of the psalm that Jesus quoted from the cross and its implications for their own faith journeys.
- Trust more deeply in God's presence and care.
- Reach out to those who feel abandoned or forgotten.

BIBLICAL FOUNDATIONS

It was nine o'clock in the morning when they crucified him. The inscription of the charge against him read, "The King of the Jews." And with him they crucified two bandits, one on his right and one on his left. Those who passed by derided him, shaking their heads and saying, "Aha! You who would destroy the temple and build it in three days, save yourself, and come down from the cross!" In the same way the chief priests, along with the scribes, were also mocking him among themselves and saying, "He saved others; he cannot save himself. Let the Messiah, the King of Israel, come down from the cross now, so that we may see and believe." Those who were crucified with him also taunted him.

When it was noon, darkness came over the whole land until three in the afternoon. At three o'clock Jesus cried out with a loud voice, "Eloi, Eloi, lema sabachthani?" which means, "My God, my God, why have you forsaken me?" When some of the bystanders heard it, they said, "Listen, he is calling for Elijah." And someone ran, filled a sponge with sour wine, put it on a stick, and gave it to him to drink, saying, "Wait, let us see whether Elijah will come to take him down." Then Jesus gave a loud cry and breathed his last. And the curtain of the temple was torn in two, from top to bottom. Now when the centurion, who stood facing him, saw that in this way he breathed his last, he said, "Truly this man was God's Son!"

Mark 15:25-39

SUGGESTED LEADER PREPARATION

- Carefully and prayerfully read Mark 15:25-39, making notes of whatever grabs your attention most, sparks new questions, or prompts new insights. If desired, consult a trusted Bible commentary.
- Carefully read "Chapter 3: My God, My God" in *Seven Words*. Note any material you need or want to research further before the session.
- Have on hand a variety of Bible translations and trusted study Bibles and commentaries for participants to use (recommended). You will need at least two different translations of Mark 15:25-39. Also have on hand a markerboard or flip chart.
- If using the DVD, preview the session 3 segment and choose the best time in your session to view it.
- If you choose to do the "Optional Activity," look up the hymn "There Is a Balm in Gilead"; be ready to share the words or a link.

AS YOUR GROUP GATHERS

Welcome participants. Ask those who attended the previous session to talk briefly about what in it most interested, challenged, or helped them.

Invite participants to use their cell phones to look up definitions of the word "godforsaken." (Alternatively, you may bring a dictionary with you, or look up definitions provided by online dictionaries and have them ready.) Ask people to read the various definitions they find and compare them. Invite discussion on these questions:

- Have you ever been to a place that might be considered godforsaken? Where was it? What was it like? What made the place seem godforsaken?
- The word usually is used to express something or somewhere that is miserable or depressing. But what would a place be like that was literally forsaken by God?
- Put yourself in the place of someone who felt they had been forsaken by God. How would you feel?

Draw attention to Susan Robb's description in chapter 3 of a time when she felt godforsaken and angry with God.

Ask:

- Was there ever a time in your life when you felt forsaken by God? Have you ever felt angry with God? Were you able to express those feelings to God? to others? (Invite people to share, but be sensitive to those who may feel reluctant to speak on this point. If no one offers an answer, be prepared to discuss a time in your own life when you felt that God was far away.)

Tell participants that this session invites us to explore what seems to be the lowest point in Jesus's life—a point at which he is willing to quote from a scripture in which the psalmist feels forsaken by God. Based on the rest of the Gospels, this is not something we might expect Jesus to say. And yet, by examining the psalm beyond the verse that Jesus quotes, we may gain greater insight into what Jesus was thinking and feeling—and hear what he is saying to us about our own relationship with God.

Pray this prayer, or one in your own words:

Lord, you know the thoughts of our hearts even before we bring them to you. You know that there are times when we feel far away from you, as if you have abandoned us. Give us the faith to always feel your presence, so that through us others may feel your presence, too. Amen.

BEING BRUTALLY HONEST WITH GOD

Ask:

- When you think of the Psalms, what kinds of sentiments come to mind for you? What kinds of feelings are commonly expressed?

Acknowledge responses and write them down on a markerboard or flip chart for all to see. Discuss some of the responses people offer (for example, psalms of thanksgiving, psalms that express God's majesty, psalms of comfort and God's protection). Invite participants to share some of their favorite psalms, or verses they remember from the Psalms, that express these sentiments. If no one volunteers, be prepared to read aloud three short psalms:

- Psalm 8
- Psalm 23
- Psalm 100

Then invite participants to think of psalms also as a way of expressing feelings of abandonment, isolation, and even anger. Read these psalms together.

- Psalm 6
- Psalm 10
- Psalm 13
- Psalm 137

Ask:

- Where in these psalms did you find feelings of despair?
- Where did you find feelings of anger? (Draw attention to the end of Psalm 137, in which the Israelites in exile asked God to kill the children of their Babylonian oppressors.)
- Were you surprised to see some of these feelings expressed in prayers to God?
- Where in these psalms did you notice prayers by individuals? Where did you notice prayers offered by the whole community?

- Have you ever felt sentiments like these that you were reluctant, uncomfortable, or embarrassed to offer up to God in prayer? Why?

Discuss:

- The Psalms show us that we can approach God, who already knows what is in our minds and hearts, with whatever we are feeling.

THE HUMAN JESUS

Say:

- While Jesus was divine—fully God—Christians believe that Jesus also was fully human, with the full range of human needs and feelings. The humanity of Jesus is never more fully on display than in his anguished words from the cross, "My God, my God, why have you forsaken me?"

Discuss:

- While we acknowledge that Jesus is both fully human and fully divine, some Christians may nevertheless find it disconcerting to see Jesus's humanity expressed in a statement that sounds as if it could be from a human being who is struggling with his or her faith in the midst of trials and suffering. Do you find it disconcerting to hear words like this from Jesus? Do you find it reassuring? Explain.
- Early Christians affirmed Jesus not only as our Lord and our Savior but also as our brother. Have you ever considered Jesus as a brother? What aspects of Jesus's humanity revealed in the Gospels guide you toward thinking of Jesus as a brother?

THE REST OF THE PRAYER

Remind participants that Jesus knows the Psalms well. He speaks the first line of Psalm 22—"My God, my God, why have you forsaken me?"—

but he knows that this prayer ends very differently from what you might expect based on its early verses. When Jesus speaks these final words from the cross, he has in mind the entire prayer, not just the beginning.

Invite a volunteer to read Psalm 22:1-18.

Ask:

- How are the words of these verses appropriate for what Jesus is feeling on the cross?
- How do you think early Christians, when reading this psalm, saw Jesus in them?

Now, invite another volunteer to read the rest of Psalm 22 (vv. 19-31).

Ask:

- How does the entire feeling of this psalm change when you continue to the end?
- Did you notice this pattern in some of the other psalms of despair that we read earlier?
- How does reading the entire psalm change how you see Jesus's prayer from the cross? What is he really saying?
- How do you interpret the psalmist's statement in verses 30-31, that future generations will say that the Lord "has done it"?

OPTIONAL ACTIVITY

In chapter 3 of *Seven Words*, Susan Robb provides the biblical context behind the African American spiritual "There Is a Balm in Gilead," then notes how the hymn turns Jeremiah's original verses of despair and abandonment into a song of hope and faith amid suffering and unrelenting racial violence and oppression. As a group, read Jeremiah 8:18-22. Then read the words to "There Is a Balm in Gilead."

Discuss:

- What are the theological outlook and message of Jeremiah's words?

- What are the outlook and message of the words of the hymn?
- What does it say about the faith of those who sang this hymn at a time when racial justice seemed like a nearly hopeless cause?
- What does this hymn say about how we experience God's presence (or feel God's absence) as a community? Why is it important to affirm that these words apply to communities as well as to individuals?
- What does this hymn have to say to us in a time when true racial justice often can seem so far away?
- Susan Robb writes that "racism denies the sovereignty of God." How so? How does "There Is a Balm in Gilead" assert God's sovereignty?

CLOSING ACTIVITY

Jesus's words from the cross remind us that prayer was a constant part of his life, that many of those prayers came from the Psalms, and that the Psalms allow us as individuals and as communities to express our deepest pains and anxieties to God. They also affirm God's presence with us.

Ask someone in the group to read Psalm 139:1-12:

> O LORD, you have searched me and known me.
> You know when I sit down and when I rise up;
>   you discern my thoughts from far away.
> You search out my path and my lying down,
>   and are acquainted with all my ways.
> Even before a word is on my tongue,
>   O LORD, you know it completely.
> You hem me in, behind and before,
>   and lay your hand upon me.
> Such knowledge is too wonderful for me;
>   it is so high that I cannot attain it.
>
> Where can I go from your spirit?
>   Or where can I flee from your presence?
> If I ascend to heaven, you are there;
>   if I make my bed in Sheol, you are there.

35

If I take the wings of the morning
    and settle at the farthest limits of the sea,
even there your hand shall lead me,
    and your right hand shall hold me fast.
If I say, "Surely the darkness shall cover me,
    and the light around me become night,"
even the darkness is not dark to you;
    the night is as bright as the day,
for darkness is as light to you.

Now, ask another member of the group to read from Paul's letter to the Christians of Rome:

Who will separate us from the love of Christ? Will hardship, or distress, or persecution, or famine, or nakedness, or peril, or sword? As it is written,

"For your sake we are being killed all day long;
    we are accounted as sheep to be slaughtered."

No, in all things we are more than conquerors through him who loved us. For I am convinced that neither death, nor life, nor angels, nor rulers, nor things present, nor things to come, nor powers, nor height, nor depth, nor anything else in all creation, will be able to separate us from the love of God in Christ Jesus our Lord.

Romans 8:35-39

Invite them to respond to these questions:

- In the coming week, where will you take up your cross?
- How will you help someone who is struggling with a heavy burden?
- How will you show God's presence for someone who feels isolated and "godforsaken"?

Close this session by praying these words, or some of your own:

O God, at times when we feel that you have forsaken us, remind us in our struggles that you have already shown us how our journey to the cross will end. You have shown the world that when human hate, human anger, human prejudice, and human violence have done their worst, your love, which never departs from us, has the final word in our lives and in human history. Give us the faith to let your love see us through, and to mirror that love to others. Amen.

Session 4
Woman, Here Is Your Son

Session Goals

This session's reading, discussion, reflection, and prayer will equip participants to:

- Explore and affirm the important role of women in Jesus's ministry.
- Recognize the symbolic role of Jesus's mother in a new creation—the church.
- Respond to Jesus's continuing call for his followers to be a new kind of family, defined by belief and practice rather than blood, tribe, or geography.
- Embrace others through our actions as brothers and sisters in Christ.

Biblical Foundations

Meanwhile, standing near the cross of Jesus were his mother, and his mother's sister, Mary the wife of Clopas, and Mary Magdalene. When Jesus saw his mother and the disciple whom he loved standing beside her, he said to his mother, "Woman, here is your son." Then he said to the disciple, "Here is your mother." And from that hour the disciple took her into his own home.

John 19:25-27

While he was still speaking to the crowds, his mother and his brothers were standing outside, wanting to speak to him. Someone told him,

"Look, your mother and your brothers are standing outside, wanting to speak to you." But to the one who had told him this, Jesus replied, "Who is my mother, and who are my brothers?" And pointing to his disciples, he said, "Here are my mother and my brothers! For whoever does the will of my Father in heaven is my brother and sister and mother."

Matthew 12:46-50

SUGGESTED LEADER PREPARATION

- Carefully and prayerfully read John 19:25-27 and Matthew 12:46-50, making notes of whatever grabs your attention most, sparks new questions, or prompts new insights. If desired, consult a trusted Bible commentary.
- Carefully read "Chapter 4: Woman, Here Is Your Son" in *Seven Words*. Note any material you need or want to research further before the session.
- Have on hand a variety of Bible translations and trusted study Bibles and commentaries for participants to use (recommended) and a markerboard or flip chart.
- If using the DVD, preview the session 4 segment and choose the best time in your session to view it.
- Prepare the candle that you will light during the activity in the "As Your Group Gathers" section.

AS YOUR GROUP GATHERS

Welcome participants. Ask those who attended the previous session to talk briefly about what in it most interested, challenged, or helped them.

As an opening activity, have the participants stand in a circle, at arm's length from each other. Light a candle and place it in the middle.

Say:

- One of the early Christian monks in the Sinai Desert found a simple way to teach people how we relate to God and each other, and we are going to re-enact it here.

Explain to the group that the candle in the center of the circle represents God. Now, ask each participant to take three steps back. Ask someone to note how this changed where each of them is in relation to God. How did it change where they are in relation to each other? Now, have the participants return to their original positions. Then ask them to take three steps closer to the candle. As they moved closer to God, how did this affect where they stood in relation to each other?

Say:

- From the cross, Jesus called us into a different and closer way of being with each other. If we lean in and listen, we will find that this way of being also brings us closer to God.

Pray this prayer or one of your own:

O God, sometimes we separate ourselves as your children from each other based on artificial constructions, in ways that we have learned from our culture rather than from you. We forget that when we separate ourselves from each other, we separate ourselves from you. Open our eyes, our minds, and our hearts so that we may see the ways you draw us together. Amen.

LIVING IN 'INTERESTING' TIMES

Using the following questions, guide your group in a discussion of how difficult times also create possibilities for growth and change. If you have a large group, consider forming smaller teams to discuss these questions, and then have one person from each group bring the points or examples raised in their conversation back to the larger group.

- In the beginning of chapter 4 of *Seven Words*, Susan Robb notes some of the ways that the COVID-19 pandemic of 2020 changed the way people lived. Describe some ways in which the pandemic disrupted your life. In what ways did these disruptions make your life more difficult?
- Did any of the disruptions actually improve your life? If so, in what ways? Were you surprised by these ways that your life became better or more satisfying?

- *Seven Words* alludes to an ancient Chinese saying that is considered a curse: "May he live in interesting times." How might "interesting times" represent a curse?
- In what ways are we living in "interesting times"?
- As Susan Robb quotes in the book, Robert Kennedy told white university students in South Africa that they lived in "times of danger and uncertainty; but they are also the most creative of any time in the history of mankind." Where do you see people creating positive change in this time of fear and uncertainty?
- In his Day of Affirmation speech, Kennedy challenged students to have the moral courage to work for change. He said, "Each time a man stands up for an ideal, or acts to improve the lot of others, or strikes out against injustice, he sends forth a tiny ripple of hope, and crossing each other from a million different centers of energy and daring, those ripples build a current which can sweep down the mightiest walls of oppression and resistance."* Where do you see ripples of hope? Where are you making ripples?

THE WOMEN NEAR JESUS

Using the following questions, guide your group in a discussion of the role of Jesus's mother and other women in the redemption of human beings. Draw participants' attention to what Susan Robb says about the way John's Gospel begins, harking back to the way the Bible begins in Genesis to present Jesus's coming in human flesh as a second, bold act of creation by God. Read aloud these verses from John's prologue:

> *In the beginning was the Word, and the Word was with God, and the Word was God. He was in the beginning with God. All things came into being through him, and without him not one thing came into being. What has come into being in him was life, and the life was the light of all people. The light shines in the darkness, and the darkness did not overcome it. . . .*

---

* Robert F. Kennedy, "Day of Affirmation Address at Cape Town University" (speech), June 6, 1966, Jameson Hall, Cape Town, South Africa, transcript, *American Rhetoric*, page updated December 22, 2019, https://www.americanrhetoric.com/speeches/rfkcapetown.htm.

To all who received him, who believed in his name, he gave power to become children of God, who were born, not of blood or of the will of the flesh or of the will of man, but of God.

John 1:1-5, 12-13

Discuss:

- From Matthew, Mark, and Luke, we know the name of Mary. But as Susan Robb points out, John's Gospel never refers to her by name, only as the "mother of Jesus." Surely, the writer of John knew Mary's name. Why do you think he refers to her only as Jesus's mother? How might this omission connect to Robb's suggestion, building on John's obvious references to the Creation story, that Mary in some ways is like a second Eve, who was "the mother of all living"?
- How is Jesus like the second Adam?
- Among Jesus's followers, according to John's Gospel, except for the "Beloved Disciple" all of those who came to the cross as witnesses were women. Why do you think this was the case? What does this suggest to you about the contribution of women to Jesus's movement?
- Like Mary, "the disciple whom Jesus loved" is never mentioned by name in John's Gospel. But this disciple and the mother of Jesus are called into a family relationship by Jesus as he hangs from the cross. For John, what is the significance of a new family in which a "mother" and "son" are not referenced by name? What do you think John wants us to understand?
- What does Susan Robb suggest about why these two are not mentioned by name but defined instead by their relationship to Jesus?

A NEW FAMILY

Using the following questions, guide your group in a discussion of the new kind of "family" that Jesus calls into being.

41

- When Susan Robb highlights the passage in which John's Gospel says that those who believed in Jesus gained the power to become children of God, she capitalizes the word "OF." How does this change in emphasis change or add to the meaning of what it is to be a child of God?

- Earlier in his ministry, Jesus kept right on teaching when told that his mother and brothers were waiting outside and wanted to see him. Then he said, "My mother and my brothers are those who hear the word of God and do it" (Luke 8:19-21; see also Matthew 12:46-50). How might this statement have seemed shocking and disrespectful to Jesus's family? How might it have seemed shocking to those in the audience?

- What do you think Jesus was trying to say about what it means to be family?

- Where have you seen or experienced relationships between people who were not biologically related but provided you with new insight into what it means to be family?

- Why do you think Jesus defines family by action (whose who do the will of God) rather than purely by belief?

- Susan Robb notes that the Gospels make no mention of the risen Jesus appearing to his biological family but only to his followers. Had you ever wondered about that before? Why do you think the Gospels recall only Jesus's appearances to those who followed him?

- How, according to Susan Robb, is Jesus redefining what it means to be the "assembly" (*ekklesia*) of all the people?

- John's Gospel tells us that Jesus did not simply instruct the Beloved Disciple to treat Jesus's mother as his own mother. John wants us to know that, from then on, the disciple took Mary into his home (we can only presume that Joseph, Jesus's father, has died and that Mary is now a widow). What does John want us to understand about the Beloved Disciple's response to Jesus's call?

- How does Jesus's call to the Beloved Disciple help you understand your own calling to discipleship?

ONE IN CHRIST

As Susan Robb explains, the early church embraced Jesus's call to become a new kind of family. Read the following passages and discuss how each one illuminates this early Christian understanding of family.

- Acts 4:32-37
- Acts 6:1-7
- Acts 10:17-36
- Romans 12:1-5
- 1 Corinthians 12:12-26
- Matthew 25:31-40

Discuss:

- What, according to these early Christian scriptures, does it mean to be "the body of Christ"?
- How does living into this call to be Christ's body shape the way our church carries out its mission and witness?
- Where, in your opinion, does our church need to live more fully into what it means to be Christ's body?
- How does living into this call shape your own life and understanding of your faith? Where do you need to live more fully into this calling?
- In what ways does Jesus's invocation of a new kind of family still have radical implications for our society today?
- In what ways does a moment of upheaval in our society create new possibilities for us, individually and collectively, to live into Jesus's way of being family?
- We speak of disruptive technologies or products that change the way people live. Jesus spoke of disrupting the way people thought of being family and being in community. What if we thought of our church as a "disrupter" in our community? What would it disrupt? How might it change the way people live? How might it change the way we think of ourselves as a church family?

CLOSING ACTIVITY

Remind participants that this is a Lenten study—a time to remember that Jesus calls us, as his disciples, to take up our own cross and follow him. Invite them to respond to these questions:

- In the coming week, where will you take up your cross?
- Where will you be "family" to others in a new and different way?

Say:

- The apostle Paul wrote that in Christ there is neither slave nor free, Jew nor Greek, male nor female. In other words, all of the distinctions created by the wider world do not apply within Christian communities.

  Invite participants to add to this list by completing this sentence:

  In Christ there is neither _____ nor _____.

Write responses on a markerboard or flip chart for all to see. Give everyone a chance to contribute.

Then ask:

- How did this list give you new insight into what it means to be the church?
- How does it challenge us to change so that we can more fully live into Jesus's call to be a different kind of family?

As a group, read aloud the words to the hymn "In Christ There Is No East or West" on the following page. (You may wish to distribute copies of it and invite participants to take turns reading the individual stanzas.)

Pray this prayer or one of your own:

Lord, make us one. Help us remember, every moment of every day, that you told us the world will know that we are your disciples by the love we show to our brothers and sisters, the members of the new family you called us to be. Give us the courage to follow you and to love without counting the cost. Amen.

IN CHRIST THERE IS NO EAST OR WEST*

In Christ there is no east or west,
In him no south or north,
But one great fam'ly bound by love
Throughout the whole wide earth.

In him shall true hearts ev'rywhere
Their high communion find;
His service is the golden cord
Close binding humankind.

Join hands, disciples in the faith,
Whate'er your race may be!
Who serve each other in Christ's love
Are surely kin to me.

In Christ now meet both east and west,
In him meet south and north,
All Christly souls are one in him
Throughout the whole wide earth.

---

* "In Christ There Is No East or West" (John Oxenham, 1908), Hymnary.org, https://hymnary.org /text/in_christ_there_is_no_east_or_west_oxenh.

Session 5
I AM THIRSTY

SESSION GOALS

This session's reading, discussion, reflection, and prayer will equip participants to:

- Reflect on the full humanity of Jesus as evidenced by his words from the cross.
- Explore the meaning and nature of "living water" and how Jesus represents living water for his followers.
- Recognize how Christians came to understand Jesus's acceptance of the "cup of suffering" also was an act of "pouring himself out" on behalf of humanity.
- Explore how their own journey through Lent calls them to be living water poured out for others.

BIBLICAL FOUNDATIONS

After this, when Jesus knew that all was now finished, he said (in order to fulfill the scripture), "I am thirsty." A jar full of sour wine was standing there. So they put a sponge full of the wine on a branch of hyssop and held it to his mouth.

John 19:28-30

He came out and went, as was his custom, to the Mount of Olives; and the disciples followed him. When he reached the place, he said to them, "Pray that you may not come into the time of trial." Then he withdrew from them about a stone's throw, knelt down, and prayed,

"Father, if you are willing, remove this cup from me; yet, not my will but yours be done."

Luke 22:39-42

Suggested Leader Preparation

- Carefully and prayerfully read John 19:28-30 and Luke 22:39-42, making notes of whatever grabs your attention, sparks new questions, or prompts new insights. If desired, consult a trusted Bible commentary.
- Carefully read "Chapter 5: I Am Thirsty" in *Seven Words*. Note any material you need or want to research further before the session.
- Have on hand a variety of Bible translations and trusted study Bibles and commentaries for participants to use (recommended) and a markerboard or flip chart.
- If using the DVD, preview the session 5 segment and choose the best time in your session to view it.
- Have paper or plastic cups on hand for everyone in your group.
- Have enough copies of the Wesleyan Covenant Prayer (contemporary version) to distribute to participants.

As Your Group Gathers

Welcome participants. Ask those who attended the previous session to talk briefly about what in it most interested, challenged, or helped them.

Invite participants to get out their cell phones and do an internet search for images of springs of water. Ask them to choose an image to share with the group and to explain why they chose that particular image.

Ask:

- Susan Robb describes her memories of a spring near her childhood home, where the water was always cool and refreshing. What memories, if any, can you share of a running spring?
- What comes to mind when you think of springs? What qualities do you associate with them?

- What do springs symbolize for you?

Say:

- In this session, we will consider how Jesus's words from the cross help us better understand him as a source of living water, how he poured himself out on our behalf, and what that means both for us and for our calling as disciples who are on our own journey to the cross.

Pray this prayer or one of your own:

Lord, you taught that those who thirst for righteousness are blessed, because they will be filled. Let us seek you today as the source of living water that will never leave us thirsty again. And make us vessels of your love, mercy, and justice that we freely pour out to those around us. Amen.

CONSIDER JESUS'S HUMANITY

In chapter 5 of *Seven Words*, Susan Robb emphasizes Jesus's humanity—something, she says, that it's easy for Christians to forget when they consider the miracles he performed. John's Gospel, from which this fifth utterance from the cross is drawn, makes Jesus's divinity unmistakably clear, both in its opening words and in Jesus's frequent "I am" sayings ("I am the way, and the truth, and the life" [John 14:6]; "I am the gate" [10:9]; "I am the good shepherd" [10:11]; "I am the resurrection" [11:25]), which echo the Hebrew name for the divine, YHWH ("I am"). Yet in the words "I am thirsty," John also shows us Jesus's full humanity, his human needs and feelings. Elsewhere in the Gospels, we see other illustrations of Jesus's humanity.

As your group prepares for this discussion, read together these passages:

1. Matthew 4:1-2 (Jesus experiences hunger)
2. Matthew 8:18-20 (Jesus desires to escape the ever present crowds)
3. John 11:32-35 (Jesus weeps when he sees Mary's grief over the death of her brother Lazarus)

4. Luke 19:41-42 (Jesus weeps over Jerusalem)
5. Luke 22:39-42 (Jesus asks to be spared from the cup of suffering)

Discuss:

- As Susan Robb notes, some Christian traditions, rejected as heretical teachings, claimed that Jesus only appeared to be human and did not really die on the cross. Why do you think some Christians might have struggled with the idea of a Jesus who was fully human as well as fully divine?

- The prologue to John's Gospel describes Jesus's identity in this way: "The Word [that is, the Mind and Spirit of God] became flesh and lived among us" (John 1:14). Why do you think that God chose to experience life on human terms, among human beings?

- How does Jesus's humanity alter your understanding of his life and mission, compared to thinking of Jesus as purely divine?

- In what ways might a fully human Jesus seem easier for you to relate to?

- In what ways might a human Jesus seem more difficult to relate to?

OPTIONAL ACTIVITY

Read aloud the account of Jesus's death from Mark 15:16-37. Before you begin, ask the participants to imagine Jesus's physical feelings and human emotions during the events described in the text. After you have read the passage together, have participants describe these feelings and emotions, and record them on a markerboard or flip chart for all to see.

Ask:

- How do these human feelings add to your understanding of God?
- How do they add to your understanding of the relationship between God and human beings?

SPIRITUAL THIRST AND LIVING WATER

As Susan Robb notes in chapter 5, the Scriptures use the image of a flowing spring of water in both the Old and New Testaments. Read together these passages that she references and others that use this imagery:

- Exodus 17:1-7
- Psalm 42:1-8
- Ezekiel 47:1-12
- Isaiah 55:1-13
- Amos 5:21-24
- Revelation 22:1-5

Discuss:

- What does flowing water symbolize in these passages? What do you think we are meant to understand about these images?

Now, read together passages in which Jesus describes himself as living water:

- John 4:10, 13-14
- John 7:37-39
- John 6:35

Discuss:

- How would you define living water?
- How do the Old Testament passages we read a few moments ago add to your understanding of what Jesus meant when he described himself as living water?
- List some of the products you have seen that are advertised to us as offering satisfaction. How do they promise to satisfy? How believable are their promises? Why do you think people believe them?
- What are you thirsty for that cannot be satisfied by ordinary water (or by something that you can buy)?

- Susan Robb writes that, in Jesus's day, people were thirsty for justice, thirsty for freedom from oppression, thirsty to be valued. What do you think people in your community are thirsty for today? Why are they thirsting?

- As Susan Robb explains, John Wesley, the founder of the Methodist movement, understood the deep quenching of our souls' thirst as sanctification—a transformative process of becoming perfected in love as the Holy Spirit works within us. Just as Jesus turned ordinary water into good wine for a celebration, Jesus's Spirit turns ordinary people into living water. How do you think that water displays itself in our lives as Christ works in us and through us? What does it look like?

THE PASSOVER LAMB

Explain:

- As Susan Robb points out, John's Gospel makes the connection between Passover and Jesus's crucifixion even more explicitly than the other Gospels. Following the other Gospel narratives, we traditionally observe Good Friday as the day of Jesus's death. But John places Jesus's crucifixion on Thursday, the day when lambs were being slaughtered for the Passover celebration, which began the next evening. John also observes that the sponge holding the sour wine offered to Jesus on the cross was lifted up to him on a hyssop branch—the same type of branch into which lamb's blood was dipped and smeared on doorposts before the first Passover.

Use this background to discuss the following questions.

- Why does John want us to connect Jesus to Passover?
- How does the occurrence of Jesus's arrest and crucifixion at Passover, rather than at some other time of the year, offer you new insights into Jesus's action and mission?

THE OUTPOURING

Use the following questions to discuss how the understanding of Jesus as living water connects to his sacrifice on the cross—and to our own calling as disciples.

- In his Letter to the Philippians, Paul says that Jesus "emptied himself" (Philippians 2:6-7). Then, in his Second Letter to Timothy, he writes, in the belief that he is near the end of his life, that he is "being poured out as a libation" (2 Timothy 4:6). Why do you think Paul used that particular phrase? How does it help you understand what Jesus did? How does this metaphor that implies Jesus is a cup or a vessel connect to the understanding of Jesus as a source of living water?
- Sometimes coaches tell their players to "leave it all on the field" or "leave it all on the court"—meaning to give everything they have and hold nothing back. Do you ever wonder why more sermons don't contain that same message for Christians? How might the church be different if that were a regular exhortation to believers?
- How are you called to pour yourself out?
- How is your church community seeking to pour itself out?
- Where are your missed opportunities to be living water for those who are thirsty?

CLOSING ACTIVITY

Distribute paper or plastic cups to each person in the group.

Say:

- On the night that he was betrayed, Jesus took a cup of wine and said, "This is my blood that is shed for you." Whenever we partake of communion together, we remember how Jesus poured himself out for us. But Jesus also calls on us to be cups for others—cups that may share living water with someone who is thirsty, cups of self-sacrifice that we pour out for others with no expectation that they can repay us.

Now, distribute copies of the Wesleyan Covenant Prayer on the following page and read it aloud together as a group.

Remind participants that this is a Lenten study—a time to remember that Jesus calls us, as his disciples, to take up our own cross and follow him. Invite them to respond to these questions:

- In the coming week, where will you take up your cross?
- To whom will you offer living water this week?
- On whose behalf will you pour yourself out?

Close the session by praying this prayer or one of your own:

Lord, we come to you thirsting for the living water you offer to us, for the peace that surpasses understanding. Open our hearts to the working of your Spirit, so that they become so overflowing with your love that we cannot contain it within ourselves. Make us like springs that gush forth to refresh others in hope and to quench the thirst of those around us. Amen.

Exchange signs and words of peace with one another as the group departs.

WESLEYAN COVENANT PRAYER (CONTEMPORARY VERSION)

I am no longer my own, but yours.

Put me to what you will, place me with whom you will.

Put me to doing, put me to suffering.

Let me be put to work for you or set aside for you,

Praised for you or criticized for you.

Let me be full, let me be empty.

Let me have all things, let me have nothing.

I freely and fully surrender all things to your glory and service.

And now, O wonderful and holy God,

Creator, Redeemer, and Sustainer,

you are mine, and I am yours.

So be it.

And the covenant which I have made on earth,

Let it also be made in heaven. Amen.

Session 6
INTO YOUR HANDS

SESSION GOALS

This session's reading, discussion, reflection, and prayer will equip participants to:

- Consider where they might have experienced "thin places" where heaven and earth come close together.
- Better appreciate Jesus's relationship to the Psalms and how these scriptures can inform their own prayer lives.
- Explore what it means to commit themselves into God's hands.
- Consider how the cross was God's defining revelation to human beings.
- Commit to "participating in Christ" in the work of reconciling love.

BIBLICAL FOUNDATIONS

After this, when Jesus knew that all was now finished, he said (in order to fulfill the scripture), "I am thirsty." A jar full of sour wine was standing there. So they put a sponge full of the wine on a branch of hyssop and held it to his mouth. When Jesus had received the wine, he said, "It is finished." Then he bowed his head and gave up his spirit.

John 19:28-30

It was now about noon, and darkness came over the whole land until three in the afternoon, while the sun's light failed; and the curtain of the temple was torn in two. *Then Jesus, crying with a loud voice, said, "Father, into your hands I commend my spirit." Having said this, he breathed his last. When the centurion saw what had taken place, he praised God and said, "Certainly, this man was innocent." And when all the crowds who had gathered there for this spectacle saw what had taken place, they returned home, beating their breasts. But all his acquaintances, including the women who had followed him from Galilee, stood at a distance, watching these things.*

Luke: 23:44-49

In you, O LORD, I seek refuge;
> *do not let me ever be put to shame;*
> *in your righteousness deliver me.*
Incline your ear to me;
> *rescue me speedily.*
Be a rock of refuge for me,
> *a strong fortress to save me.*

You are indeed my rock and my fortress;
> *for your name's sake lead me and guide me,*
take me out of the net that is hidden for me,
> *for you are my refuge.*
Into your hand I commit my spirit;
> *You have redeemed me, O LORD, faithful God....*

Be gracious to me, O LORD, for I am in distress;
> *my eye wastes away from grief,*
> *my soul and body also.*
For my life is spent with sorrow,
> *and my years with sighing;*
my strength fails because of my misery,
> *and my bones waste away.*

I am the scorn of all my adversaries,
> *a horror to my neighbors,*
an object of dread to my acquaintances;
> *those who see me in the street flee from me.*
I have passed out of mind like one who is dead;
> *I have become a broken vessel.*

For I hear the whispering of many—
terror all around!—
as they scheme together against me,
as they plot to take my life.

But I trust in you, O Lord;
I say, "You are my God."
My times are in your hand;
deliver me from the hand of my enemies and persecutors.…

Blessed be the Lord,
for he has wondrously shown his steadfast love to me
when I was beset as a city under siege.
I had said in my alarm,
"I am driven far from your sight."
But you heard my supplications
when I cried out to you for help.

Psalm 31:1-5, 9-15, 21-22

SUGGESTED LEADER PREPARATION

- Carefully and prayerfully read John 19:28-30; Luke 23:44-49; and Psalm 31:1-5, 9-15, 21-22. Make notes of whatever grabs your attention, sparks new questions, or prompts new insights. If desired, consult a trusted Bible commentary.
- Carefully read "Chapter 6: Into Your Hands" in *Seven Words*. Note any material you need or want to research further before the session.
- Have on hand a variety of Bible translations and trusted study Bibles and commentaries for participants to use (recommended).
- If using the DVD, preview the session 6 segment and choose the best time in your session to view it.

AS YOUR GROUP GATHERS

Welcome participants. Ask those who attended the previous session to talk briefly about what in it most interested, challenged, or helped them.

In chapter 6 of *Seven Words*, Susan Robb describes the island of Iona as a "thin place," where heaven and earth come so close together that there is almost no boundary between them. You may wish to search and have some images available of Iona on your cell phone or tablet to show the group.

Ask:

- For Susan Robb, the mountains of Colorado are a thin place. Where are places that make you feel especially close to God?
- What is it about those places that make you feel that way?
- Read together the description of Jesus's crucifixion from Luke 23:44-49. What makes the cross feel like a thin place? Why?

Say:

- Today, in the last of our sessions on *Seven Words*, we come to the thin place where God's love for us was defined in the ultimate act of self-giving, by God who became a human being, on behalf of all humankind.

Pray this prayer or one of your own:

O God, during these past weeks we have been on a journey together to the cross, attempting to follow in Jesus's footsteps as his disciples. You have walked with us, strengthening us, holding our hands, teaching us not to be afraid. You have given each of us a cross to carry, a cup that is ours to drink, and a mission to undertake for you. Give us the full measure of strength to see it through and the full measure of faith to commit our lives into your hands. Amen.

OUR DAILY PRAYERS

Use the following questions to lead a discussion about Jesus's relationship with the Psalms and how they can inform our own prayer lives.

- Susan Robb points out that it should be no surprise that some of Jesus's last words from the cross were prayers from the Psalms. After all, he knew the Psalms backward and forward and had surely prayed one of them, as did other Jewish children of his day, as a bedtime prayer taught to him by his parents. Can you remember any bedtime prayers or table blessings you learned as a child? What were they? What lessons did they teach?

- Do you have favorite psalms that you turn to at certain times? when you're thankful to God? when you're fearful? when you're angry? Invite participants to share these psalms.
- If God already knows the thoughts of our hearts, why can it still be helpful for us to treat these psalms as prayers? Why might we sometimes be afraid to share with God what is on our hearts?

Now, read Psalm 31 aloud.

Ask:

- Jesus quotes one line from Psalm 31, but he was familiar with the entire psalm. How did the words of this psalm speak to his situation on the cross? What insights do they give us into what Jesus was thinking, beyond the few words that he actually uttered?

PUTTING OURSELVES IN GOD'S HANDS

Use the following questions to discuss what it means to put our lives completely in God's hands.

- What holds you back from entrusting everything to God?
- How would your day feel different if, as Susan Robb asked her congregation to do, you began each morning with this prayer that echoes Jesus's final words: "God, into your hands I commit my life"?
- How could living more fully into that prayer sustain you in the days and weeks beyond Lent?
- Susan Robb writes, "'Into your hands I commend my spirit' are not words to die by. They are words that teach us how to live." How could putting your trust in God re-orient your perspective on life?

- How can you live more into Jesus's teaching to consider the lilies of the field and the birds of the air, who are liberated by God from worrying about things they cannot control?

The Ultimate Revelation

Use the following questions to discuss the cross as God's revelation of love.

- Susan Robb writes that the cross is "God's defining revelation of love so pure, so complete, that it pours itself out for us in the knowledge that love wins the victory over human fear, human hate, and human violence." As Christians, we may have been conditioned to think of Easter as God's victory and the cross as something sad and shameful. How is the cross in and of itself a victory? What was won?
- In writing the First Letter to the Corinthians, the apostle Paul acknowledges in chapter 1 that the cross is a stumbling block (v. 23) for many who cannot comprehend that God's Messiah could have been crucified on a Roman cross. In what ways is a crucified Messiah, in the apostle Paul's phrase, "the power of God" (v. 18) to those who are being saved? In what ways might this idea still be a "stumbling block" for some?
- How did the cross, in Paul's words, make "foolish the wisdom of the world" (v. 20)?

Participating in Christ

Use the following questions to discuss what it means to participate with Christ in the transformation of the world.

- As Susan Robb explains, the Greek word used in John's Gospel for Jesus's sixth utterance from the cross is *tetelestai*, which "describes something that is completed but has ongoing, far-reaching implications for the future." In what ways was Jesus's mission accomplished on the cross? In what ways is it ongoing?

- Susan Robb notes that for Paul, to be "in Christ" (2 Corinthians 5:17-19) is "to participate in Christ." What is the work in which we are participating?
- How does the idea that we are "participating" in Christ help you feel empowered as a disciple?
- How does "participating in Christ" give you an added feeling of responsibility as a disciple?

CLOSING ACTIVITY

Read aloud the final sentences from chapter 6 of *Seven Words*:

During this Lenten season, as you draw closer to the cross, may you find a thin place where heaven and earth intersect and where you can experience the hands of the living God guiding your life, lifting you up, drying your tears. Most of all, may God bless your hands *and* feet as you answer the call to take up your cross and follow where Jesus has walked, sowing seeds of the Kingdom along the way. And may God grant you the faith to pour yourself out in love, for all of your life, until you are able one day to complete your mission and to say, as a faithful servant, "Into your hands, Lord, I hand over my spirit."

Ask:

- How has our study helped you better understand your calling as a disciple to take up your cross and follow Jesus?
- Where have you felt God's hand holding you?
- How has our study given you new insight into who God is and God's will for your community of faith at this time?

Remind participants that this is a Lenten study—a time to remember that Jesus calls us, as his disciples, to take up our own cross and follow him. Invite them to respond to the following questions.

Ask:

- In the coming week, where will you take up your cross?
- As you approach the cross, how will you seek out one of the spiritual "thin places" where heaven and earth draw close together?
- How will you let God use you as a canvas this week to paint a work of love, grace, mercy, and justice?
- What seeds will you plant for God this week?

Thank everyone for having taken part in the study.

Close the session by praying this prayer or one of your own:

Lord, you have taught us every day to sow cross-shaped seeds of love, justice, forgiveness, and reconciliation. Give us the faith to trust our lives to you, to pour ourselves out in love, and to complete the mission you have given us. Amen.

Exchange signs and words of peace with one another as the group departs.

Made in United States
Orlando, FL
04 March 2022

15385875R00037